MARTYRS, ROGUES & WORTHIES

SONGS & TUNES FROM SCOTLAND IN THE CELTIC TRADITION

COMPOSED AND ARRANGED BY
ALAN REID
OF BATTLEFIELD BAND

Kinmor Music

ACKNOWLEDGEMENTS

Cover and layout design: **John Slavin**/Living Tradition
Cover Photograph: **Cailean MacLean**, Isle of Skye

I used **FINALE 3.21** and **FINALE 2000** music software for this book
and I heartily endorse it.

A special thanks to my friends **Matthew Hynes** and **Ian Rough** who spent
hours poring over my crotchets, quavers, ties and counting the beats.
Another special thanks to my family, **Mary, Morven** and **Curstaidh**, who
endured my numerous one-way conversations with the computer, not all of
them polite, and tolerated every advance and setback in compiling this tome.

© Kinmor Music 2001

1st Edition - March 2001

Printed by:
Meigle Printers, Block II, Units I & II Tweedbank Industrial Estate, Galashiels. TD1 3RD

Published by:
Kinmor Music, Shillinghill, Temple, Midlothian. EH23 4SH
Tel: 01875-830328 • email: kinmor@templerecords.co.uk

ISBN 0 9540160 0 9

FOREWORD

This book represents twenty-five years of travelling the world with Battlefield Band. As a band we began to introduce our own tunes into our repertoire fairly early on. The songs came later. Brian McNeill came up with a great song 'The Lads O' The Fair' for our 'Home Is Where The Van Is' album on Temple Records, and it was then that it occurred to me to try my hand at songs as well.

The first song of mine that the band used was 'The Dear Green Place' a song about the history of Glasgow. An ambitious subject, and for the most part I have since been more modest in my horizons. Some of the songs in this volume have been triggered by something I've read, like 'Ballantrae' or 'Darien'. Others have been the result of sitting down with a piece of paper, writing down a line, and seeing what my imagination throws up, as with 'The Green And The Blue' or 'Jenny O' The Braes'. Others like 'The Bonny Jeannie Deans' or 'Jock The Can' have been prompted by childhood memories. With some songs I've forgotten how they came to be written, and that, I guess, is part of the mystery of songwriting.

Most of the songs and tunes are transcribed into the keys in which they were performed. A few, I've moved up a tone or down a semi-tone to make them more guitar or fiddle friendly. Some of the song structures are more complicated than simply verse/chorus/verse so I've endeavoured to set them out in as clear a way as possible. The guitar chords are there as a reference point only and are not set in stone. I've also included a couple of pieces which show the left hand for the keyboard. These are compositions where I feel the left hand is an important part of the music, and of course are only of interest to keyboard players.

I have to thank all the great singers and musicians that I've worked with in 'Battlefield Band' for all the help and wonderful memories they've given me. I've been very fortunate to be part of a great band that's become somewhat of an institution, and whose many former members include players still making significant contributions to this great musical tradition of ours which has devotees and friends all around the world.

I have always tried to write songs that tell stories, and compose melodies that stay with you. I hope you readers will find songs and music that give you pleasure and encourage you to give voice or lift that whistle to your lips.

Alan Reid - December 2000

SONG INDEX

	Page
A Chance As Good As Any	27
Ballantrae	25
Campbell's Sisters	36
Christ Has My Hart Ay	11
Darien	22
Fifty Four Winters	18
Five Bridges To Cross	12
I Am The Common Man	6
Iolaire Na Mara (The Sea Eagle)	10
Jenny O' The Braes	1
Jock The Can	19
Just A Boy	16
Lady Kilmarnock's Lament	5
Love No More	30
Mary Morison	14
Miner's Wives	7
My Home Town	24
Rantin' Rovin' Robin	15

Same Old Story	26
Shining Clear	20
The Arran Convict	9
The Bonny Jeannie Deans	17
The Dear Green Place	3
The Devil's Courtship	35
The Devil Uisge Beatha	34
The Green And The Blue	28
The Hoodie Craw	32
The Image O' God	8
The Lass O' Glencoe	37
The Pleasure Will Be Mine	2
The Riccarton Tollman's Daughter	21
The River	33
The Straw Man	23
The Tail O' The Bank	4
Tramps And Hawkers	13
Up And Waur Them A' Willie	31
Whit Can A Lassie Dae?	29

Discography - 55

SONGS FROM SCOTLAND IN THE CELTIC TRADITION

TUNE INDEX

A' Chlach Uaine (The Green Stone)	(air)	40		Let There Be Drams	(reel)	54
Angst Agus Angus	(jig)	50		Mary Cassidy	(air)	39
Atlantic Bridge	(waltz)	48		Norman MacAskill of Lochinver	(march)	52
Brodick Castle	(air)	40		Pinky, Porky and Jim	(jig)	49
Cumbernauld House	(air)	43		Renaldo The Rebounder	(jig)	51
Curstaidh's Farewell	(air)	42		She's Late But She's Timely	(air)	38
Falkland Palace	(minuet)	44		Something For Jamie	(air)	45
Feiger's Warning	(march)	47		The Cumbernauld Perennials	(march)	46
Gledstane's March	(march)	50		The Million Dollar Sweetie	(jig)	47
Goat Fell	(air)	43		The Sleeping Warrior	(air)	41
Jam Tomorrow	(reel)	54		The Wilton Street Dawdle	(hornpipe)	38

Discography - 55

TUNES FROM SCOTLAND IN THE CELTIC TRADITION

JENNY O' THE BRAES

Alan Reid
© Kinmor Music

1. The people cried her Jenny o' the braes
   And she was weel kent tae us a',
   Her ganglin' body stickin' oot her claes
   Made her staun oot when she strode doon the braes.

2. Twa days a week she'd come visitin' the toon,
   She'd tak the braes, rain, hail or shine.
   Her silver hair wid be fleein' in the win'
   And folk thocht her a creature mad or wild.

3. When ice and snow gripped a' the country ,
   Ye'd see the smoke rise frae her chimney.
   The world ablow could then rest easy
   For Jenny o' the braes.

4. The wind blew a' weys roon the muir.
   It rattled on her cottage windae.
   She sat inside close by the fire.
   She was content in her ain company.

5. And if ye asked her if she was weel
   She'd say "Ah'm grand, sir, how's yersel?"
   And then she'd trudge on up the hill,
   Jenny o' the braes.

6. She wisnae bothered ower want o' gear,
   She lived on cheese, breid, oats and barley.
   She wisnae fashed wi' trouble or care,
   She'd spurn the knock that brocht a helpin' hand

7. Sometimes she'd wander ower the muir
   Collectin' heather plants and floo'ers
   And singin' softly tae hersel,
   Jenny o' the braes.

8. Last year she bided mair at hame,
   Her cottage door was seldom open.
   And when the Spring floo'ers cam' tae bloom
   She hardly ever ventured doon the braes.

9. One day when someone was out walkin'
   They saw her chimney wisnae smokin'
   They fun' her sittin' in the kitchen,
   A smile upon her face,
   Jenny o' the braes.

A song about someone on the outside edge of society. Jenny is a relic of a dying age, where misfits are still looked out for by the local community.

On **'RAIN, HAIL OR SHINE'** - *See Discography*

THE PLEASURE WILL BE MINE

Alan Reid
© *Kinmor Music*

Chorus
If ye come wi' me tae Fintry
Willie says to Caroline
I wid hae a happy heart
The pleasure will be, mine she says
The pleasure will be mine

1. The rain was fa'en doon sae hard the drains were overflowin'
   Ye'd almost think the Flood was comin' on
   So they sheltered in a corner tryin' to keep oot a' the water
   And he told her a' the things he had in mind

2. The paper says the workforce will be laid off efter Christmas
   There's a downturn in the business so they say
   I'll no' sit aboot here waitin' on some company decision
   So on Friday I'll be liftin' my last pay

3. We can pack oor bags and leave this place and tak the road tae Fintry
   For the country air's as sweet as guid red wine
   And when summer comes aroon again and corn is ripe for getherin'
   We'll find out if ma notion's right or wrang

4. They walked hand in hand and wandered down beside the sleepy river
   Where the city sounds grew distant in their ears
   The moonbeams in the water glinted silver as he kissed her
   And the rumble of the city disappeared

• Myself with Davy Steele and Rob Van Santé our sound engineer, during our '98 tour of Australia.

A song about moving. I was trying to write a lyric that is not set in any particular time.

On **'LEAVING FRIDAY HARBOR'** - *See Discography*

THE DEAR GREEN PLACE

Alan Reid
© *Kinmor Music*

For my first serious attempt at songwriting. I chose a fairly modest subject, the entire history of Glasgow! The rest of the lads were very patient with me as I spent months wrestling with the lyrics, lurching towards a workable version.

On 'ON THE RISE' - See Discography

1. It was by the clear Molindinar burn
   Where it meets and runs with the river Clyde,
   And they tell the tale of the holy one
   Who was fishing down by the river side,
   A holy man, from Fife he came,
   His name they say was Kentigern,
   And by the spot where the fish was caught
   The dear green place was born

2. Now the salmon ran through the river stream
   And they salted them by the banks o' Clyde
   And the faces glowed as the silver flowed
   And the place arose by the riverside,
   There was cloth to dye and hose to buy,
   The traders came from miles around
   And they raised a glass to the dear green place,
   The place that was a town

   Chorus
   There is a town that once was green and a river flowed to the sea,
   The river flows forever on but the dear green place is gone

3. When the furnaces came to fire the iron
   And folk were thrown from the farmland

Then the Irishman and the Highlandman
And the hungry man came with willing hands
They wanted work, a place to live,
Their empty bellies needed filled,
And the farmyard was another world
From the dirty, overcrowded mill

4. Now you may have heard of the foreign trade
   And fortunes made by tobacco lords,
   But the working man slaved his life away
   And an early grave was his sole reward.
   A dreary room, a crowded slum,
   Disease and hunger everywhere,
   And the price to pay was another day
   To fight the anger and despair

5. A thousand years have been here and gone
   Since Kentigern saw the banks o' Clyde,
   How many dreams and how many tears
   In a thousand years of a city's life?
   A city hard, a city proud,
   And no mean city it has been.
   Perhaps tomorrow it yet may be
   The dear green place again

1. The sunset falls behind the Kyles and Cowal hides the light
   And the dark hills lie against the sky like sentries in the night,
   Along the Firth to the Holy Loch the lights are shining bright
   As we stand across the water at the Tail o' the Bank

2. Our fathers stood here yesterday and gazed upon the Firth
   On those old familiar liners sailing from their place of birth
   And the salt, sea air embraced them as they stood upon that earth
   And they dreamed of better fortune for the Tail o' the Bank,
   Better fortune for the Tail o' the Bank

3. We have seen the emigration boats departing with the tide,
   We have heard the dying echoes of the shipyards on the Clyde
   And the promises of those who said that they were on our side
   Lie stranded like a shipwreck on the shoreline

4. There are faces you remember, there are some you soon forget,
   There are places that won't leave you, never mind how far you get,
   But wherever there's a hungry heart a spark is living yet.
   Aye and that's what keeps them goin' at the Tail o' the Bank,
   The folk at the Tail o' the Bank, That's what keeps them goin'
   The folk at the Tail o' the Bank.

Greenock is an ancient port, on the Firth of Clyde once famed for shipbuilding, and now trying to cope, like much of Scotland in a post-industrial climate. From the hills above the town there is a wonderful panorama of the Firth of Clyde and the Kyles of Bute, which, set against the town's bleak landscape, was the juxtaposition providing the idea for this song.

On **'CELTIC HOTEL'** - See Discography

LADY KILMARNOCK'S LAMENT

words: traditional
music: Alan Reid
© Kinmor Music

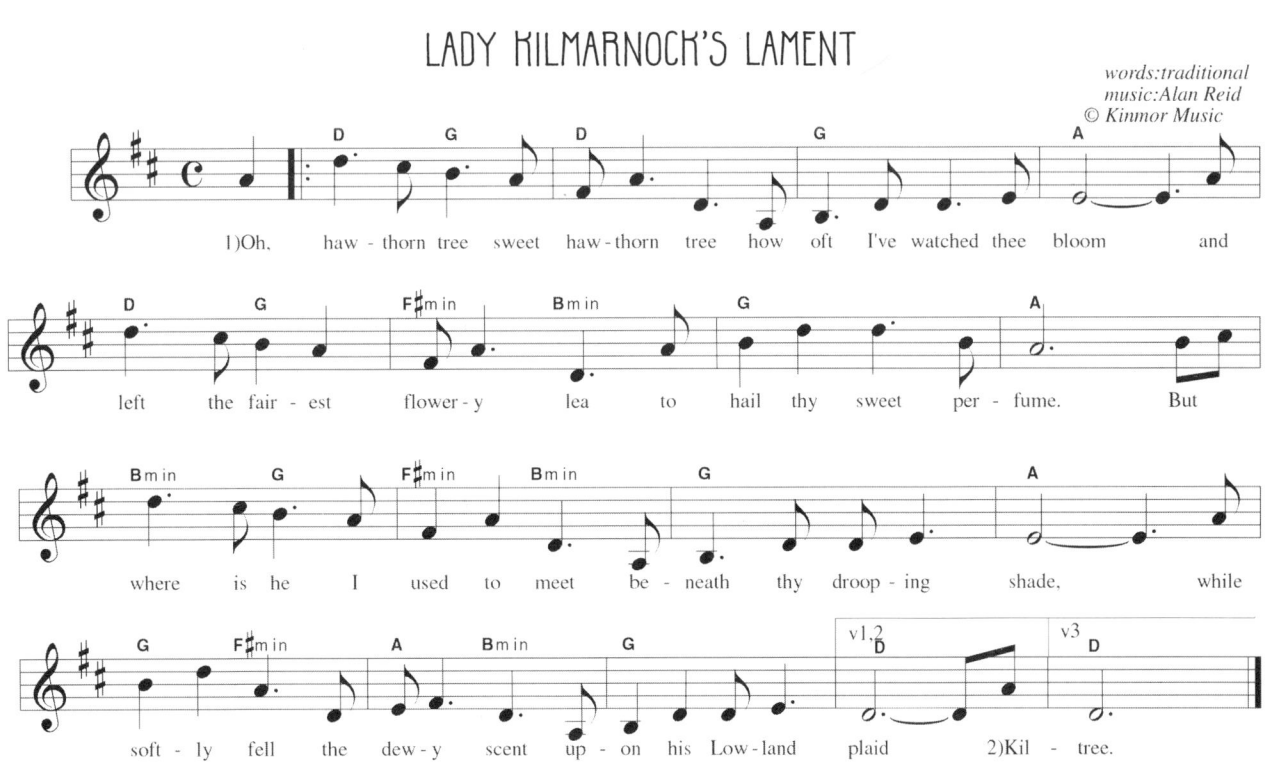

1. Oh hawthorn tree, sweet hawthorn tree, how oft I've watched thee bloom
   And left the fairest flowery lea to hail thy sweet perfume.
   But where is he I used to meet beneath thy drooping shade
   While softly fell the dewy scent upon his Lowland plaid

2. Kilmarnock sought me for his bride, a noble brave and free,
   What were a jewelled crown beside the love he gave to me
   I loved and was beloved again, no blyther bride could be
   But now in sorrow I remain beneath the hawthorn tree

3. Oh hawthorn tree, sweet hawthorn tree, no more I'll hear him sing
   The loyal songs he sang to me on Scotland's royal king
   My lord upon a scaffold fell for Scotland and for me
   So here I lie, just like to die, beneath the trysting tree

I found the words of this song in a book some years ago (I forget which book). Lord Kilmarnock supported Charles Edward Stewart, the young Pretender, in the 1745 rebellion and was beheaded for his trouble.

I AM THE COMMON MAN

words: Joe Corrie
music: Alan Reid
© Kinmor Music

1. I am the common man (I am the fool, the despised)
   I am the common man (I am the brute and the slave)
   I am the common man (I am a tool in their eyes)
   I am the common man from the cradle to the grave,
   From the cradle to the grave

2. I am the common man (I am the hewer of coal)
   I am the common man (I am the tiller of soil)
   I am the common man (I am the serf of the seas)
   I am the common man born to bear and to toil
   Born to bear and to toil

3. I am the common man but masters of mine take heed
   For you have put into my head many wicked deeds

4. I am the builder of hall, I am the dweller of slums,
   I am the filth and the scourge when depression comes,
   When winter's depression comes

5. I am the fighter of wars, I am the killer of men.
   Not for a day or an age but again and
   Again and again and again and again and again

6. I am the common man, born to bear and to toil

This song, and the following one (Miner's Wives), were recorded by 'Battlefield Band' and segued together on the album 'Anthem For The Common Man'. The words were written by Joe Corrie, a Fife miner in the 20's who began writing poetry and eventually gave up mining to become a playright and poet. I set the words to music after gaining the kind permission of Joe's daughter Morag. His poems made a powerful impression on me and were always well received by our audiences.

On 'ANTHEM FOR THE COMMON MAN' - See Discography

MINERS' WIVES

words: Joe Corrie
music: Alan Reid
© Kinmor Music

1. We have borne good sons to broken men,
   Nurtured them on our hungry breasts
   And given them to our masters
   When their day of life was at its best.

2. We have dried their clammy clothes by the fire,
   Nurtured them, cheered them, tended them well
   Watched the wheels raising them from the mire
   And watched the wheels lowering them tae hell.

3. We have prayed for them in a godless way,
   We never could fathom the ways of God,
   We have sung with them on our wedding day,
   Knowing the journey and the road.

4. We have stood through the naked night
   To watch the silent wheels that raised the dead.
   We have gone before to raise the latch
   And lay the pillow beneath their head

5. We have done all this for our masters' sakes,
   Did it in rags and did not mind.
   What more do they want, what more can they take
   Unless our eyes and leave us blind?

Another Joe Corrie poem which the Batties played together with 'I Am The Common Man'. The song speaks for itself.

On 'ANTHEM FOR THE COMMON MAN' - See Discography

THE IMAGE O' GOD

words: Joe Corrie
music: Alan Reid
© *Kinmor Music*

1. Crawlin' aboot like a snail in the mud,
   Covered wi' clammy blae,
   Me made efter the image o' God,
   Is that no' laughable tae?

2. Howkin' away at a mountain o' stane,
   Gaspin' for want o' air,
   The sweat makin' streams doon ma bare back bane
   And ma knees are hackit and sair

3. Strainin' and cursin' the hale nicht through
   Half starved, half blin', half mad
   And the gaffer he says less dirt in that coal
   Or ye go up the pit ma lad

4. So ah gie ma life tae the Nimmo squad
   For eicht and fower a day,
   Me made efter the image o' God
   Is that no laughable tae?

5. Wi' the muck in ma nails and a lung fu' o' dust
   Ah work in the dark a' the day.
   So pardon me then if ah don't gie a smile,
   Ah'm made in his image, ye say.

• **Myself and Ian MacDonald posing by the Taj Mahal during our tour of India in 1992.**

This is the first of Joe Corrie's poems I set to music, a caustic jibe at the idea of God casting man in his image set against the squalid conditions of the miner.

On **'THERE'S A BUZZ'** - *See Discography*

THE ARRAN CONVICT

Alan Reid
© Kinmor Music

Chorus
I wish I was back on the the Lochranza ferry
With long-legged Mary,
Breathin' the spray and the sweet island air of the morning.
But I'm wastin' away in this swelterin' prison, the mercury's risin'
And freedom's a dream that arrives and escapes with the dawnin'.

1. It seems just like yesterday sailin' from Brodick,
   Across the Atlantic in search of a wife and some land.
   But the New Brunswick winters are lonely and hard
   So I followed the wagons out west with no money or plan

2. I worked on the railroad with Chinese and Irish,
   I slept in the pinewoods and heard the wolf creep to the door.
   But a Scotsman in Portland took all of my money,
   He sold me a cartload of candles he'd robbed from a store

3. And I fell in wi' gangsters and dealers in moonshine
   And soon they involved me in drivin' their wagons of booze.
   One night we were ambushed and I killed a black man.
   Now I'm in the jail house and one of the hard labour crews.

4. Sometimes when it's dark I remember Lochranza
   And days when the rain from Kintyre was a sheet without end
   And long-legged Mary who smiled at me slyly
   And when they release me I think I'll go back there again

I wrote this song shortly after we spent a holiday in the beautiful island of Arran. I was surprised to learn that the Highland Clearances had touched Arran as well, it being so far south. This, coupled with knowledge that a group of religious islanders emigrated to Canada in the nineteenth century gave me the 'meat' for this song, although it was actually triggered by me sitting down with a piece of paper and writing down the line 'I wish I was back on the Lochranza ferry'.

On '**THREADS**' - *See Discography*

This song had a long gestation period. I wrote the melody many years ago and had words which included 'Homewards again, homewards again'. I abandoned that set of lyrics, then a long time after I read a novel called 'The Stonor Eagles' by William Horwood and also heard a radio programme about the re-introduction of sea eagles to Scotland. From that broadcast I gleaned a lot of information from John Love of the Countryside Commission who was instrumental in bringing these great birds back to Scotland. It was he who quoted the beautifully poetic Gaelic 'Iolaire Suil Na Greine', the eagle with sunlit eye.

On **'THE SUNLIT EYE'** - *See Discography*

1. The great beating wings leave the ocean behind.
   They head for the land, the rocks and the sand
   And a mad howl of gulls rise to cry to the wind
   Iolaire na mara is home in the islands again

2. There's puffin to harry and eider to stalk.
   There's fish and there's deer, there's fulmar and auk
   The eyrie is far from the prying of man
   and Iolaire na mara is home in the islands again
   Homewards again, homewards again,
   Iolaire na mara is home in the islands again

3. For sixty long years he was banished and gone.
   They plundered his nest, they hunted him down.
   But now from the land of the fjords he's returned
   And Iolaire na mara is home in the islands again
   Homewards again, homewards again,
   Iolaire na mara is home in the islands again

4. The white tail flies high, the white tail flies free.
   He rides with the wind, over land, over sea
   And when the sun sets in the west once again
   There's a light in his eye, 'Iolaire suil na greine'

5. His friends are the mountains, the mist and the wind.
   His kingdom the sky, the sea and the land.
   He wanders the loch side, the hill and the glen.
   He's lord of the northland and
   Iolaire na mara is home in the islands again
   Homewards again, homewards again.
   With a spread of his wings and a tug of the wind
   Iolaire na mara is home in the islands again
   Homewards again, homewards again,
   Iolaire na mara is home in the islands again

CHRIST HAS MY HEART AY

traditional carol
music : Alan Reid
© *Kinmor Music*

1. For us that precious bairn was born
   For us he was baith rent and torn
   For us he was crownit with thorn
   Christ has my hart, ay
   Christ has my hart, ay

2. For us he shed his precious blood
   For us was nailet on the rood
   For us in mony battle stood
   Christ has my hart, ay
   Christ has my hart, ay

3. Next him to love his mother fair
   With steadfast hart for evermair
   She bore the birth, freed us from care
   Christ has my hart, ay
   Christ has my hart, ay

> I found the words of this ancient Easter carol in a history of 'The Scottish People' by T. C. Smout. The words were so old and so simple, yet so eloquent, I resolved to put a tune to them. The recording on 'Stand Easy' album remains one of Battlefield Band's more unusual pieces of music.

On **'STAND EASY + PREVIEW'** - *See Discography*

FIVE BRIDGES TO CROSS

Alan Reid
© Kinmor Music

1. Now Winter is drawin' its cloak o'er the North
   And the sky over Sutherland's heavy and grey,
   The birds o' the summer long gone to the south
   And night time is fallen to darken the day.
   The hill folk that lately have come to the coast
   Sit quiet and hungry and chilled to the bone
   The leaving has weakened the old ones the most
   The fire in their bellies has gone.

   Chorus
   Five bridges to cross,
   The Bonar, the Ness, the Tay and the Forth.
   The first bridge is the hardest of all,
   The one to decide if you stay or you go.

2. No woodsmoke at morning nor beasts to be fed,
   No rest on the hill as you take your noon bread,
   And no call of the curlew to beckon you home
   Nor drink with your neighbour at evenin'.
   This town disappears in a blanket of grey
   When the haar at the dawn slithers in from the sea
   And the smell of the hill seems a lifetime away
   And there's no soul abroad in the evenin'.

3. Some say you'd be better to wait for the Spring
   And some say the fishin' will come back again
   For the fickle white herrin' will surely return
   To bring health and good cheer in the mornin'.
   But others contend that delay is a crime
   And that fortune won't favour the timid, the blind
   For there's no pot of gold for those waitin' behind
   Just the long weary game of survivin'.

Five Bridges to Cross
This song is about the suffering of the hill folk in Sutherland during the time of the Clearances.

On **'THE SUNLIT EYE'** - See Discography

Tramps and Hawkers
I reworked this fine old traditional song by adding a first and last retrospective verse to make the core of the song a dream sequence. Fancy that now.

On **'THREADS'** - See Discography

TRAMPS AND HAWKERS

words: trad./Reid
music/trad.
© Kinmor Music

1. I dreamred a dream the other night, a dream of long ago.
   I saw yin o' the travellin' folk along the open road.
   His step was light, his head held high to catch the scent o' Spring
   And his voice rang roon the countryside as he began to sing

2. Oh come a' ye tramps and hawker lads, ye getherers o' blaw
   That tramps the country roon an' roon, come listen yin an' a'
   I'll tell tae you a rovin' tale o' sights that I hae seen
   Far up intae the snowy north and south by Gretna Green

3. I've travelled roon the Lothian lands, I've seen the rushin' Spey
   I've been by Crieff and Callender and by the shores o' Loch Tay
   I've watched the rain on the Border hills, the mist in Northern Glens
   And I've bedded doon beneath the moon in corries naebody kens

4. And I'm often doon by Gallowa' and roon aboot Stranraer
   My business takes me onywhere sure I travel near and far
   For I've the rovin' in ma blood and there's nothin' that I lack
   As long as I've my daily fare and claes upon ma back

5. I'm happy in the summertime beneath the bricht, blue sky
   Ne'er thinkin' in the mornin' at nicht whaur I will lie
   Barn or byre or onywhere or oot among the hay
   And if the weather does permit I'm happy every day

6. And I think I'll go tae Paddy's land, I'm makin' up ma mind
   For Scotland's greatly altered noo', I cannae raise the wind
   And I will trust in Providence if Providence proves true
   And I will sing of Erin's Isle when I return to you

7. Come a' ye tramps and hawker lads, ye getherers o' blaw
   That tramps the country roon an' roon, come listen yin an' a'
   I'll tell tae you a rovin' tale o' sights that I hae seen
   Far up intae the snowy north and south by Gretna Green

8. When I'd awoken from my dream the dawn song had begun
   The birds sang out their old, old songs to greet the risin' sun
   I lay among the shadows and I thought of days long gone
   And those wanderin' tramps and hawker lads whose days are surely done

MARY MORISON

Robert Burns, arr. A. Reid
© *Kinmor Music*

1. Mary at your window be,
   It is the wished, the trysting hour.
   Those smiles and glance let me see
   That make the miser's treasure poor.
   How blythely would I bide the stour,
   A weary slave frae sun tae sun,
   Could I the rich reward secure,
   The lovely Mary Morison.

2. Yestreen when to the the trembling string
   The dance gaed through the lichtit ha'
   To you my fancy took its wing
   I sat but neither heard nor saw.
   Though this was fair and that was braw
   And yon the fairest o' the toon,
   I sighed and said among them a'
   Ye arnae Mary Morison.

3. Mary can you wreck his peace
   Wha for your sake wid plainly dee?
   Or can you break that hert o' his
   Whase only faut is lovin' ye?
   If love for love ye cannae gi'e
   At least be pity to me shown.
   A thocht ungentle cannae be,
   The thocht o' Mary Morison.

Mary Morison was one of the many ladies Robert Burns admired, and perhaps it even developed to more than admiration

On **'THE SUNLIT EYE'** *- See Discography*

• Myself with John McCusker, Mike Katz and Karine Polwart. Taken prior to our first tour with Karine in 2000.

RANTIN', ROVIN', ROBIN

Robert Burns tune: Dainty Davie
Robert Burns, arr. A.Reid
© Kinmor Music

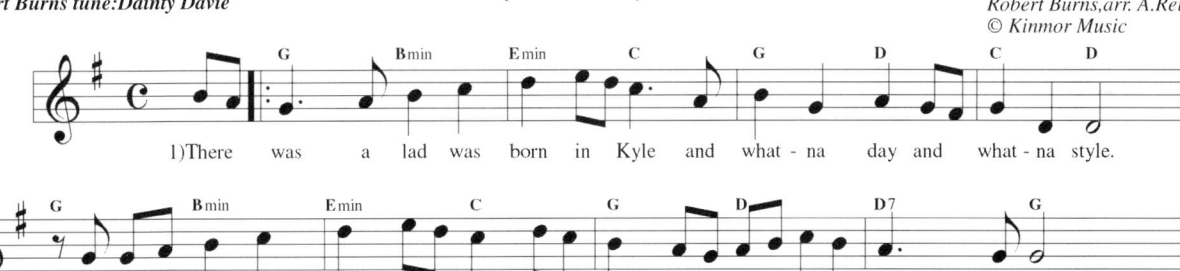
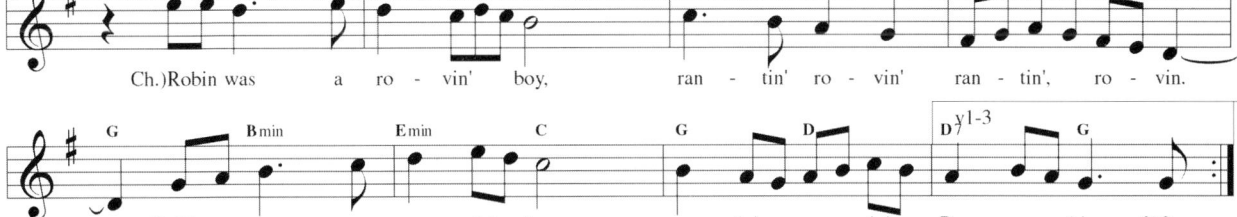

1. There was a lad was born in Kyle
   On whatna day and whatna style
   A doot it's hardly worth the while
   Tae be sae nice tae Robin

   Chorus
   Robin was a rovin' boy,
   Rantin' rovin', rantin' rovin'.
   Robin was a rovin' boy,
   Rantin' rovin' Robin

2. Oor monarch's hindmaist year but yin
   Was five and twenty days begun
   'Twas then a blast o' Januar win'
   Blew hansel in on Robin

3. He'll hae misfortune great and sma'
   But aye a hert abune them a'.
   He'll be a credit tae us a'.
   We'll a' be proud on Robin

4. As sure three times three maks nine
   I swear on ilka score and line.
   This lad will surely love oor kind
   So leeze me on me Robin

• This photo of Brian McNeill, Duncan MacGillivray and myself was taken in 1979.

A song where the bard measures himself and his life, sung to the tune of 'Dainty Davie'.

On **'THE SUNLIT EYE'** *- See Discography*

JUST A BOY

Alan Reid
©*Kinmor Music*

1. Oh love of mine when we were first as one
   I thought that I was strong enough for anything.
   A look, a touch from you and I would turn
   And follow like a little clockwork toy.
   The grass grew tall and fast before I saw it grow,
   The ketlle whistled long before I even heard it blow,
   And all the while I thought that I was in control
   But now I know that I was just a boy.

2. The candle lights the sparkle in your eyes
   Reminding me of diamonds I am looking for.
   I stumble on through quicksands and through fires
   And all the while your smile lights up the day.
   The ghost of childhood dreams still haunt the older man,
   They summon discontent for all those lost, abandoned plans
   And worry is his partner come to take his hand.
   When all is said and done he's just a boy.

3. The wool, the tweed, the leather I will don
   To keep me warm when winter winds are howling.
   I would not care for me if you were gone.
   Without you there is nothing to enjoy.
   Though plastic cards and paper seem to take me far
   And hustlers try to catch my eye and seek to bend my ear.
   All that's dear to me awaits behind one door
   To welcome home the one that's still a boy.
   And though that flush of youth is gone for evermore
   To you I know this one is just a boy

This is a song I wrote with all us older lovers in mind.
On **'THE SUNLIT EYE'** - *See Discography*

THE BONNY JEANNIE DEANS

Alan Reid
© *Kinmor Music*

1. This is the story o' the bonny Jeannie Deans,
   She was a paddle steamer built in Govan.
   She left her slipway in 1931
   Tae serve at Craigendoran.
   Throughout her days on the Firth o' Clyde
   She plied her trade wi' grace and charm,
   She won the hearts o' sailin' men
   Fae Arrochar tae Arran.

   Chorus
   And she would waltz around the Kyles,
   Her paddles turning, the waters churning,
   A trail of foam upon the brine
   As braw as ony o' the Queens,
   She was the bonny Jeannie Deans

2. My name is William Geddes I was once her engineer,
   They said for fun that I would race the seagulls.
   I tellt the Captain the Jeannie was a star
   So we challenged a' her rivals.
   She took them on and outran them all
   And brought me joy and great satisfaction.
   I called the firemen to leave the coal
   And join in celebration.

3. On summer days you would often see her sail
   The coastal waters as far as Paddy's milestone.
   Her mighty engines were always polished fine
   And perpetually in motion.
   In Winter time she would be repaired
   And painted up for the coming season
   And in the Springtime she'd reappear
   Steamin' out o' the horizon.

4. The day arrived upon the Firth of Clyde
   The Jeannie Deans made her last departure.
   She went tae London and then she was retired
   Tae Antwerp and the breakers.
   The Jeannie Deans may well be gone
   But she's remembered in a' the harbours.
   We'll never see her like again
   Come sailin' in these waters.

> The golden age of the Firth of Clyde paddle steamers was from the early years of the last century to the 1960's. These steamers carried generations of folk from Glasgow and the west of Scotland to their favourite resorts on the Clyde coast. The 'Jeannie' was perhaps the best loved. I sailed on her when I was about eight years old and she made an impression that I've never forgotten.

FIFTY FOUR WINTERS

Alan Reid
© Kinmor Music

1. Fifty four winters the auld yin sat here
   At his place in his corner and suppin' his beer
   And he hasnae been seen for a fortnight or mair
   And we don't know the reason why
   He regaled any one that would listen tae him
   O' his sodgerin' days when he wis a young man
   And the times he served in the Italian campaign
   He wid tell wi' a gleam in his eye

   Chorus
   In the streets and piazzas they stood and they cheered
   And they waved as the sodgers passed by
   In the vineyards and olive groves people appeared
   Grazie mille Scozzesi they cried
   Under the blue of the Mediterranean sky

2. He was born in the shade o' a Lanarkshire hill
   That was cut and ripped open tae haul out the coal
   Only kent o' the pit and the bing and the shale
   Never dreamed o' the world outside
   But that world went tae war when he'd just left the school
   So he went doon the mine and he waited a while
   Until he was an age he could join the Argylls
   And they taught him to march and to fight

3. He saw action below the North African sun
   He was calm under fire, he was good with a gun
   By the time he'd left Sicily he was a man
   Wi' a taste for ragazze and wine
   And later that year he was sent back again
   And they fought all the way to the Northern plain
   And the dark heavy clouds o' his Lanarkshire hame
   Seemed a lifetime away in his mind

4. And when he came back hame at the end o' the war
   He stepped off o' the train and straight intae this bar
   And ever since then he has never strayed far
   And the world has been passing him by
   So for fifty four Winters he sat in his chair
   And relived all his glories and times in the war
   And all o' this time we have never been shair
   If his story's the truth or a lie

For some people war is the highlight of their life. In this story the soldier cannot adjust to the drudgery of peacetime and looks for solace in drink and the past.

JOCK THE CAN

Alan Reid
© Kinmor Music

1. Now the wind is howlin' along the shore
   And there's an auld man that shuffles along,
   Jock the Can, him that knocks on the auld wives' doors,
   And he tells them he'll gie them a song.
   Noo Jock was a fine young lad afore he went tae the war
   But when he came back fae the fightin' he wisnae the same lad.
   Now he's jist an auld man that's wandered and gone
   Aye he carries the can and he's wandered and gone

2. Jock the Can would sing ye an auld song
   And when he'd done he would gie ye his can
   He would stand just waitin' for somethin'
   Like a drink or a copper or two in his hand
   There's them that ignored auld John and other yins chased him tae hell
   And some took him in for a bit o' a meal, "sit doon by the fire, John
   For your jist an auld man that's wondered and gone
   Aye ye carry the can and ye're wandered and gone"

3. Now the children they a' laughed at John
   For they thought him a silly auld man
   And they knew he wis different fae other folk
   He'd nothin' at a' except for his can.
   Sometimes he'd a drink in him and he staggered aboot in the rain
   And people would say what a helluva shame, he's naebody tae help him,
   But he's jist an auld man that's wandered and gone,
   Aye he carries the can and he's wandered and gone.

4. In the parish there's still a few auld yins
   Can remember Jock the Can
   And they smile when they talk o' the auld days
   And that daft auld shell o' a man
   But they say it's a' different now, everybody's the same
   And they tell ye they think it's a helluva shame, there's naebody like him now.
   Him that carries the can, he's dead and he's gone
   Auld Jock the Can, him and his kind they are gone

> Jock is an amalgam of characters that were quite common during my childhood, - back court singers serenading the Glasgow tenements for a few coppers and a couple of characters in Kilmarnock, 'Wee Boabby' and 'Jock Foy'. Wee Boabby used to hurl his bogey (a wee cart) along the main thoroughfare from one end of Kilmarnock to the other, for no apparent reason. Jock was an alcoholic down and out who hailed anyone who came near him.
> I was a bit scared of him and asked my mum what was wrong with him. She replied somewhat mysteriously that he had been shell-shocked in the war and I used to wonder what that meant.

On 'CELTIC HOTEL' - *See Discography*

SHINING CLEAR

verses: Robert Louis Stevenson
chorus and music: Alan Reid
© Kinmor Music

1. A mile and a bittock, a mile or twa
   Abune the burn, ayont the law,
   Davie and Donald and Charlie and a'
   And the moon was shinin' clearly.
   Yin went hame wi' the other and then
   The other went hame wi' the other twa men
   And baith wid return him the service again
   And the moon was shinin' clearly

   Chorus
   It's oot the barn and ower the hill,
   Through the dark and there's the still.
   A cup in your hand and there's the still
   And the moon was shining clear.

2. Clocks were chappin' in hoose and ha'
   Eleeven, twelve, yin an' twa
   The guidman' face wis turned tae the wa'
   And the moon was shinin' clearly
   A wind got up fae affae the sea,
   It blew the stars as clear's could be,
   It blew in the een o' a'the three
   And the moon was shinin' clearly.

3. Noo Davie was first tae get sleep in his head
   "The best o' friens' maun twine", he said
   "Ah'm weariet and here I'm awa tae ma bed"
   And the moon was shinin' clearly.
   Twa o' them walking and crackin' their lane,
   The mornin' light cam grey and plain
   And the birds they yammert on stick and stane
   And the moon was shinin' clearly

4. Years ayont, years awa'
   Lads ye'll mind whate'er befa'
   Lads ye'll mind on the bield o' the law
   And the moon was shinin' clearly

Taken from a Robert Louis Stevenson poem to which I added a chorus and wrote the tune. It remains my only full 'collaboration' with Robert Louis Stevenson although one of his novels was the inspiration for another song (see Ballantrae). Note the last verse is only half length.

On **'THERE'S A BUZZ'** - *See Discography*

THE RICCARTON TOLLMAN'S DAUGHTER

Alan Reid
© Kinmor Music

1. As I was a' walkin' through auld Killie toon
   It was at the back end o' November
   My gaze was drawn tae a getherin' o' folk
   A' assembled by Kilmarnock Water
   In the dreich Winter's morn a game was weel begun,
   The curlin' stanes slid back and forwarts
   And the breaths like clouds floated upwards tae the skies
   Wi' the whoops and cries fae the teams o' curlers

2. My attention was drawn tae a young bonny lass
   And she stood and watched, a close observer
   My eyes were consumed as she followed all the play
   And she cheered her faither and her brother
   I ga'ed and I spoke and I tellt her my name
   And she said she was cried Jean Alexander
   She lived wi' her folk at the Riccarton toll
   And she was the tollman's only dochter

3. At the end o' the game her faither came across
   And he shook my hand and he looked me over
   He said 'Young man come and jine us on the road'
   Then he took her arm and we walked thegither
   And when we had won tae their cottage by the toll
   I wis asked inside tae drink and blether
   And that was the start o' the winnin' o' my heart
   And the coortin' o' the tollman's dochter

4. Here's a health tae the guid folk o' auld Killie toon
   The engineers and the carpet workers
   The wabsters, the coopers, the distillers o' the dram
   Their weemin folk and their sons and daughters
   And here's tae the Winter that brought us a' the snaw
   And the ice that froze Kilmarnock water
   And here's tae the curlers that brought me to my love
   The Riccarton tollman's only daughter

Curling is an ancient and enduring pastime in Scotland. I saw a great photo of folk curling in the late 1800's, in a pictorial history of Kilmarnock. The men all had cloth caps and some of them wore huge shoes called 'carpet bits'. I decided this scene should have a song.

On **'HAPPY DAZE'** - *See Discography*

1. God preserve us Provost Anderson from this burnin' black disaster
   For the justice o' the Lord is hard tae thole.
   He has wreaked an awful vengeance on our wild and reckless schemes.
   His mighty finger flicks and scatters dreams afore his mockin' gaze
   For Darien, Darien, Darien is dead.

2. The city's in a turmoil, there's a whirlwind o' rumour
   And there's panic in the eyes o' Christian men.
   This thunderbolt is quakin' every corner o' the land
   And honest guidmen wring their hands and raise their faces heavenwards
   Darien, Darien, Darien is dead

3. We trusted you John Anderson and a' your wealthy friens
   A' your fine words weaved and danced aboot oor ears
   Like a snawdrift in the desert they are vanished in the void
   It's a sair and bitter harvest that has brought us tae our knees

4. Two thousand souls departed, a nation's dream is gone
   And King William's loyal minions watched it die.
   And every wave from here to there another penny gone,

The coffers of old Scotland are bled dry and hope is barren now
Darien (The New World beckoned us)
Darien (There is no second chance)
Darien is dead (We ventured into Panama with heart and not with head)
Darien (We trusted Providence)
Darien (It has abandoned us now)
Darien is dead, Darien is dead
Darien is dead, Darien is dead
Darien is dead

> Written for the ill fated expedition to establish a Scottish colony in Panama at the end of the 17th century after Scots merchants were refused royal assent to trade in Virginia and the Carolinas. The resultant failure of the colony cost 2000 Scots lives and £500,000 Scots, the loss of which was felt the length and breadth of Scotland, and did much to force the Act of Union 1707, a tether that has only recently begun to unravel.

On **'NEW SPRING'** - *See Discography*

THE STRAW MAN

1. It's o' a certain fermtoon by Deveron's banks and bonny borders
   There lived a wife cried Mistress Grieg wha kept the servin' quines in order
   Too-ra-loo, too-ra-loo-la-laddie, too-ra-loo-ra-laddie, too-rye-ay

2. Each nicht afore she ga'ed tae bed the servin' quarters she searched over
   In case some laddie there micht hide and in among them prove a rover
   To-ra-loo etc

3. Noo these young women they grew tired o' this attention thrust upon them,
   They got together and conspired to catch the gude wife and the auld man

4. Now they set out tae get some claes, a suit was fun' and they procured it
   And made a mannie a' stuffed wi' straw and in ablow the bed they moored it

5. That nicht when Mistress Grieg cam' roon tae guard them a' fae carnal danger
   She spied ablow the curtain pan a fit belangin' tae a stranger

6. Come oot o' there ye brainless loon, tae think I cannaa see ye hidin'
   Though she wis dancin' up and doon he peyed nae heed intil her biddin'

7. She's tae the door and she's tellt the quines tae pull him oot and fling him yonder
   And bade the auld man doon the stairs tae cudgel him if he got by her

8. They've pullt him oot and they've tossed him doon, the auld man resolute and ready,
   Sae weel he laid the cudgel on the legs cam' fleein' aff the body

9. The auld wife's howled the hale place doon, the lassies' couldnae haud their laughter
   The auld man's taken tae his bed, he never rose for twa days efter

10. Noo Mistress Grieg and her gude man I trust nae mair the young folks bother
    And keep the cudgel tae thersel' or else they micht be up for murder

> A humorous song from Aberdeenshire. Mistress Grieg apparently did exist. She must have been a fearful woman.

On **'LEAVING FRIDAY HARBOR'** - *See Discography*

MY HOME TOWN

Alan Reid
© Kinmor Music

• Showing that even Battlefield Band were not immune to the vagaries of mid 80s fashion are Alistair Russell, myself, Dougie Pincock and Brian McNeill.

1. My home town, the kingdom of the wee man
   My home town, dominion o' the chip van
   My home town
   Where centuries of sweat have stained and tanned the streets and walls,
   Lined the mansions and the halls
   Where man and boy still love to watch and play the football game
   And sunset for the cowboy is the last bus hame
   It's still the same
   My home town

2. My home town, the statue and the bingo
   My home town, the wine bar and the wino
   My home town
   Where ghostly tramcars rumble through the fog of their folklore.
   Ancient chariots of yore
   Where lofty cranes stretch out and point out across the city sky
   Like standing stones they're echoes of an age gone by
   We wonder why
   In my home town

3. My home town, the singers and romancers
   My home town, the wide boys and the chancers
   My home town
   Where the midnight drunk will waltz the stage like all who came before
   He knows the script, he knows the score
   Her humour is a plague of weeds that won't die down
   She's a grand old princess looking for her long lost crown
   She won't lie down
   My home town

> This is a song which Iain MacKintosh, the Glasgow singer, recorded for his album 'Risks And Roses'. It's about our home town.

BALLANTRAE

Alan Reid
© *Kinmor Music*

[Sheet music with lyrics:
1) See the bil-lows rise and fall, ride the swell and grip the rail, sail to-wards the o-pen burst of day. Shadows race a-gainst the bow, dark-ness is be-hind you now. Up ahead the lights of Ballan-trae
3) Peo-ple say that blood is thick-er than wa-ter. Don't for-get it no matter what you do. When there's bad blood and bro-ther turns a-gainst bro-ther, people suf-fer folk like me and you]

1. See the billows rise and fall,
   Ride the swell and grip the rail,
   Sail towards the open burst of day.
   Shadows race across the bow,
   Darkness is behind you now
   Up ahead the lights o' Ballantrae.

2. See the solid Ailsa rock,
   Guardian against the waves,
   Mighty crag that keeps the hordes at bay.
   Irish hills are to the stern,
   Turn your cheeks against the wind,
   Feel the chill and look to Ballantrae.

3. People say that blood is thicker than water
   Don't forget it no matter what you do.
   When there's bad blood and brother turns against brother,
   People suffer folk like me and you

4. Voices ringing in your brain
   Call you to America.
   America's a wilderness, they say.
   Figures standing on the shore
   Wave farewell forever more
   As you turn your back on Ballantrae.

• Battlefield Band receiving a platinum disc from Norman Blake of Teenage Fanclub for the New Spring album in 1992.

This song was suggested by the Robert Louis Stevenson novel, 'The Master Of Ballantrae'. It's not meant to be a song about the book, more an evocation of the feelings which I remember from reading it, which is a long time ago. I hope it makes sense.

1. It's the same old story, Caledonia
   You take the road for glory or shut the door and the light goes out.
   Others came before me, felt your cold and rain.
   Sons and daughters turned their backs and left your hills behind.
   Trails across the wilderness to ragged hills and plains.
   Ragged bands in search of where the western winds begin
   Threads across the centuries, your children scattered far
   It's the same old story, Caledonia

2. I have made the journey, left an open door.
   I took the road for glory and I left my native shore.
   Others came out with me, for what is there to choose.
   If there's nothing for you, then there's nothing left to lose
   Trails to where the cities spring from deserts and from plains
   Where the mountains lead to oceans and the western winds begin
   Threads to where the highways and the phone lines funnel far
   It's the same old story, Caledonia

3. Every far flung corner has a dawn that creeps and falls upon
   The scattered seeds of Alba and they rise and give their labour
   To another foreign land

4. I come home a stranger, dollars in my hand.
   I see the anxious faces, it's a look I understand.
   Another generation, same old worry lines
   Gazing past my shoulder to the light on the horizon
   And those threads across the centuries in a long unbroken line
   Maybe one day they won't have to leave your hills behind
   To take the road in search of that elusive western wind
   Will you keep them satisfied so they don't wander far
   That's another story, Caledonia
   That's another story, Caledonia

A song about Scottish emigration and the mixed feelings of familiarity, alienation and 'foreignness' that the emigrant has when visiting home again.

On **'THREADS'** *- See Discography*

A CHANCE AS GOOD AS ANY

words: Brian McNeill
music: Alan Reid
© Kinmor Music

1. Oh the musket fires a bullet down its barrel black and bonny-oh
   And nane can aim sae straight and true as my boy Johnny-oh
   He fires upon the enemy, the sergeant gie's him money-oh.
   Maybe he'll come back again, he's a chance as good as any-oh

2. Oh, the fife plays sweetly, ye can hear it fine and dandy-oh
   Nane can play it half as sweet as my boy Sandy-oh
   To stop the sodgers thinkin', the sergeant thinks its handy-oh
   For its cheaper than a tot o' rum and no sae dear as brandy-oh

3. Oh, the drum beats loud o'er the rattle o' the cannon-oh
   My boy Willie beats upon it as he's standin'-oh
   The sergeant makes him beat sae hard ye'd hear the noise in London-oh
   For when they're listenin' tae the drum they's never think o' runnin'-oh

4. There's Marshalls and MacGregors, there's MacGillivrays and Mathiesons
   Bonny boys frae Bonnybridge and lucky lads frae Laurieston
   Apprentices for raw recruits and squaddies wha'd be journeymen
   If the half o' them had a job at hame ye'd never see them back again

5. Left, right, march and fight, try tae show ye're willin'-oh
   Follow the musket, fife and drum and mind ye've ta'en the shillin'-oh
   And if you sit and rue the day you listed for the government
   You can hear the sergeant laughin', for he's got you in his regiment

The lyrics of this song were written by my old Batty cohort Brian McNeill who decided to put words to a tune that I played so much he had no other choice. A good song though.

On **'THERE'S A BUZZ'** *- See Discography*

THE GREEN AND THE BLUE

Alan Reid
© Kinmor Music

Chorus
Don't turn to look on the green hills of Antrim
Fermanagh's behind you, it's time to move on
Look onwards tae Glasgow and all your tomorrows
The future lies there and it's waitin' for you
As the green crosses over to meet with the blue

1. And what was the sense when the wee ones were cryin'
   The cries of the hungry, no sense to remain.
   No prayer could recover a sister, a brother
   So farewell to Fermanagh, the prayin' is done

2. The land that you leave has had too many martyrs
   And too many lives that have perished in vain
   And too many boats sailing out from its harbours
   With cargoes that never came homewards again

3. If the wings of the eagle could carry you over
   To the land of the prairie then surely you'd fly.
   But an ocean so wide and a far, distant country
   So far from your own land is no place to die

A song highlighting the Irish emigration to Scotland, a movement of people which continues to this day.

On **'NEW SPRING'** *- See Discography*

WHIT CAN A LASSIE DAE?

Alan Reid
© Kinmor Music

1. Whit can a lassie dae?
   When the notion is upon her,
   When the laddies look her way
   But they never make an offer.
   Whit can a lassie dae?

2. Winter nichts are lang
   And it's cosy in the kitchen
   The company is fine
   So it's maybe no' surprisin'
   Whit then a lass micht dae.

3. Some may sneer and scorn,
   Sayin' spoiled by a waster,
   But wha wid want tae turn
   Intae a tight lipped, girnin' spinster,
   Whit can a lassies dae?

4. Never mind the murmurin',
   The nods, the winks, the whisperin'
   And hints o' nichts cavortin'
   Wi' the lad that minds the travellin' stallion

5. A fermtoon can be dreich
   And life was made for sharin'
   If there's no a laud for you
   You maun settle for a bairn

6. The guid Lord micht provide,
   Micht provide a wee bit son or daughter
   But you maun scrape and fight
   For yer wee bit pride and siller.
   Whit can a lassie dae?

7. Never mind the murmurin',
   The nods, the winks, the whisperin'
   And hints o' nichts cavortin'
   Wi' the lad that minds the travellin' stallion

8. Whit is done is done
   It's time tae coont yer blessins'
   Ye can loo the blethers gab
   Ye've kept the fermtoon guessin'
   Whit can a lassie dae?

A song I wrote for a playlet by the late Jessie Kesson, the great writer from Aberdeen. The story is of a young farm girl in Aberdeenshire who falls pregnant and is the object of disapproval in the community.

On **'THE SUNLIT EYE'** - *See Discography*

LOVE NO MORE

Alan Reid
© *Kinmor Music*

1. When the clouds desert the sky,
   When the rainbows lose their colour,
   When the snow falls warm and dry
   Then will I love no more,
   Love no more.

2. When the birds refuse to fly,
   When the streams restrain the salmon,
   When the bees turn from the pollen
   Then will I love no more
   Love no more.

3. When the forest spurns the deer,
   When the hare runs slow and solemn,
   When the fox forsakes his lair
   Then will I love no more
   Love no more.

4. Winter fires burn fierce and bright,
   Wild the flames and leaping high,
   Embers glowing in the night
   And dying by the day.

5. Now the corn is young and green,
   Now the barley's madly dancing,
   Down the hillside burns are rushing,
   Surely I will love again,
   Love again.

A love song I wrote a few years ago for my wife.

On **'THE SUNLIT EYE'** - *See Discography*

UP AND WAUR THEM A' WILLIE

words: traditional
music: Alan Reid
© Kinmor Music

1. When we went tae the field o' war and tae the weaponshaw
   Wi' true design tae serve oor king and chase oor faes awa'
   Lairds and Lords came there bedeen and wow gin they were sma'
   While pipers played fae richt tae left, fy furich Whigs awa'

   Chorus
   Up and waur them a' Willie. Up and waur them a'
   Up and sell your sour milk and dance and ding them a'

2. And when oor army was drawn up, the bravest e'er I saw
   We didnae doubt tae rax the rout and win the day an' a'
   Oot ower the brae it was nae play tae get a better fa'
   While pipers played fae richt tae left, fy furich Whigs awa'

3. When brawly they attacked oor left, oor front and flank an a'
   Our bold commander on the field our faes their left did ca'
   And there the greatest slaughter made that e'er poor Donald saw
   While pipers played fae richt tae left fy, furich Whigs awa'

4. First when they saw oor hielan' mob they swore they'd slay us a'
   And yet yin fyled his breeks for fear and so did run awa'
   We drove them back tae Bonnybrigs, dragoons and foot and a'
   While pipers played fae richt tae left, fy furich Whigs awa'

This song was written by James Hogg, the Ettrick Shepherd, a contemporary of Walter Scott and a fascinating individual. As well as being a writer and collector of folk songs and tales, he was a highly imaginative novelist, largely dismissed in Edinburgh literary circles as a self-educated, uncouth and eccentric Border peasant. Anyway I took the liberty of writing my own tune for this song which is one of several on the subject of the battle of Sheriffmuir (1715). By the way both sides - the Jacobites and the Hanoverians - claimed to have won this battle.

On **'HOME IS WHERE THE VAN IS'** *- See Discography*

THE HOODIE CRAW

words: Alan Reid
music: Alan Reid/John McCusker
© Kinmor Music

1. The Hoodie craw has a black, black hert, he's the vilest o' the craws.
   He's a greedy gled and an evil scavengin' thief where'er he goes.
   For he picks at the hert and he pecks at the corp
   And he drinks o' the blood o' his prey
   It's a gey ill wind in the world o' birds when the Hoodie blaws their way

2. The sick will fear him hover near for he smells their failing breath
   Where the feeble lie he'll wait nearby and attend them at their death
   He'll worry the weak wi' a jab o' his beak, he'll frighten young and old
   And the wind that blaws the Hoodie in has a cheerless, bitter cold

3. In the open sky his piercing eye will search the ground below
   And the threshing sound o' his beating wings his victims soon will know
   No clamour calls or helpless cries divert him from his task
   And the whistlin' wind that sends him in has an icy, chilly blast

4. The eagle guards his eyrie safe high up in the hills
   And the fearless robin braves the cold and damp, wet, winter chills.
   But craws gang up and hound their prey and send them tae their grave.
   And the prize they crave is the fat and the juice
   And the blood o' the Ravenscraig.
   The prize they crave is the fat and the juice
   And the blood o' the Ravenscraig (No more! No more! No more!)

5. The skin is stripped, the bones are picked, the carcass dead and gone
   And the cries that echoed round the skies are quiet and forlorn
   The rain falls down to heal the scars and wash them in its flood
   And the Hoodie rides on another wind in search of other blood.
   The Hoodie rides on another wind in search of other blood
   Ravenscraig (No more! No more!)
   Ravenscraig (No more! No more !)
   Ravenscraig (No more! No more!)
   Ravenscraig (No more!)

A song which uses allegory to illustrate a social situation, namely the closure of the Ravenscraig steelworks in Lanarkshire which finished off the steel industry in Scotland.

On '**QUIET DAYS**' - See Discography

THE RIVER

words: Alan Reid
music: John McCusker/Alan Reid
© Kinmor Music

1. Quiet days upon the river, quiet times in the shipping trade.
   No more freighters to deliver, no more tankers to be made.
   Blow of hammer gone forever, clash of metal, squeal and din.
   No more wailing of the hooter flushing out a thousand men

   Chorus
   They can't bring back this old shipbuilding,
   No returning to your father's ways.
   But these reminders by the water
   Linger on from yesterday

2. Rows of slipways stand forgotten, empty yards with rotten frames.
   Silent quays lie abandoned, they once were busy in better days.
   This old shipbuilding gone forever, no more flags on launching day.
   Days of pride and days of sorrow, were they as golden as they say?

3. Quiet days upon the river, quiet times upon the quay
   High above a seagull passes over
   Down the river and out towards the sea

Sparked by a trip down the Clyde one summer where I was struck by the huge ghostly cranes that lined either bank, monuments to an industry whose great days were long gone. John McCusker helped with the melody on this one.

On **'QUIET DAYS'** - See Discography

THE DEVIL UISGE BEATHA

words: Alan Reid
music: trad./Reid
© Kinmor Music

1. He watches for the gauger man that prowls the countryside,
   He hides his liquid treasure then waits for night and rides
   Ower the Torrance burn tae Glesca where there's plenty that will buy her,
   She's that sweet forbidden devil uisge beatha.

2. A band o' wild marauders in the colours o' Colquhoun
   Were camped among the Campsie moors above the Lennoxtoon.
   The folk below were soon tae know they were clan Gregor men
   When they came sweepin' doon the Campsie Glen.

3. They scattered a' before them, a' the weemin and the bairns.
   They chased the fermin' workers and the fermers' fae their hames
   They gethered up the cattle and they camped aside the hill
   And there they fun' the hidden whisky still

   Chorus
   Whisky is a deevil jaud that burns the brains o' man
   He'll dance or stagger, sing or fight,
   He'll argue black and blue is white
   The fermer's wife, the weeda and the weary workin' man
   They fill the air wi' curses on that devil uisge beatha

4. The Campsie men assembled then tae see what could be done
   But shepherd lads and cottars cannae match a hielan' band.
   They cursed the thievin' reivers and their heathen hielan' cries
   As they drank their fill aneath the evenin' skies

   Chorus

5. Whisky is a deevil jaud that burns the brains o' man
   For in the night the hielan' men fell drunk upon the grun.
   The Campsie men crept up to them and slew them as they lay
   And a' was back in order by the day

6. There's stills above the Clachan, there's stills aroon the fells
   There's stills aroon the countryside nae gauger man can smell.
   But the one that snared the Gregor was mair valuable than ten
   Tae the honest fermers o' the Campsie Glen

   Chorus: The last line of this chorus should be,
   They fill the air wi' blessins' on that deevil uisge beatha

NOTE:- Melody of verses 4 and 5 same as 1. Melody of verse 6 same as 3.

THE DEVIL'S COURTSHIP

words: traditional
music: Alan Reid
© Kinmor Music

1) I'll buy you a pennyworth o' priens if that be the way true love begins, if you'll gang a-lang wi' me ma dear, if ye'll gang a-lang wi' me. Ye can hae your pennyworth o' priens though that be the way true love begins for I'll never gang wi' you my love and I'll never gang wi' you.

1. I'll buy you a pennyworth o' priens if that be the way true love begins
   If ye'll gang along wi' me ma dear, if ye'll gang along wi' me

2. Ye can hae your pennyworth o' priens though that be the way true love begins
   For I'll never gang wi' you, ma dear, I'll never gang wi' you

3. I'l buy you a braw snuff box, nine times opened, nine times locked
   If you'll gang along wi' me, ma dear, if you'll gang along wi' me

4. I don't care for your braw snuff box nine times opened, nine times locked
   For I'll never gang wi' you, my dear, I'll never gang wi' you

5. I'll buy you a silken goon wi' nine stripes up and nine stripes down
   If you'll gang along wi' me, ma dear, if you'll gang along wi' me.

6. Ye can hae your silken goon wi' nine stripes up and nine stripes doon
   For I'll never gang wi' you, ma dear, I'll never gang wi' you

7. I'll buy you a nine stringed bell, tae ca' your maid whene'er you will
   If you'll gang along wi' me, ma dear, if you'll gang along wi' me.

8. I'll no hae your nine stringed bell tae ca' my maid whene'er I will
   For I'll never gang wi' you, ma dear, I'll never gang wi' you

9. I'll gi'e you a kist o' gold tae comfort you when you are old
   If you'll gang along wi' me, ma dear, if you'll gang along wi' me

10. These are sweet words you say, so mount your horse and ride away
    I'll gang along wi' you, ma dear, I'll gang along wi' you

11. They'd scarcely gaun a mile afore she spied his cloven heel
    I rue I cam wi' you, she says, I rue I cam wi' you

12. I'll grip ye hard and fast, gold won your virgin heart at last
    And I'll no' part wi' you, ma dear, I'll no part wi' you

13. And as they were gallopin' along the cold wind carried her mournful song
    I rue I cam wi' you, she says, I rue I cam wi' you

The Devil Uisge Beatha
The Devil's Courtship
Two 'Devil' songs here. *The Devil's Courtship* finds him in a familiar role of 'enticer'. This very ancient ballad and motif, must have given nightmares to generations of young women. In *The Devil Uisge Beatha* old nick takes on the form of whisky. The Gaelic phrase 'uisge beatha' literally translated means 'water of life' and was Anglicised to become the word 'whisky'. The song is about an incident around the Campsie Glen in the hills north of Glasgow. Cattle thieving Highlanders were regarded as savages by locals who demonstrated their civilised behaviour by hiding illicit whisky stills all over the place and slaughtering said savages whenever they got the chance.

On **'NEW SPRING'** - *See Discography*
On **'HAPPY DAZE'** - *See Discography*

CAMPBELL'S SISTERS

Alan Reid
© *Kinmor Music*

Chorus
You can tell there's goins' on afore ye reach the corner
Wi' the sounds o' the guitar and fiddle waftin' through the wa'
Through the windae you can see the animated faces,
Hear the banter o' the voices and the laughter in the ha'.
For the crowd that is foregethered tae partake in celebration
Is assembled here fae a' the airts tae jine the fun an' games
And like honey bees they swarm aboot the centre o' attraction
And it's Campbell and his sisters comin' hame.

1. Maggie is the youngest one, wi' admirers by the dozen,
   Laughs at a' their antics as they follow her aroon.
   Tryin' like haddies right enough, fendin' aff their pals and cousins,
   Lassies fairly tak the huff when Maggie comes tae toon.

2. Morag is the clever miss, educated at the college,
   Eloquent in French and Spanish, sweary words an ' a'
   Whirls like a Dervish when she's dancin' at the ceilidihs
   Where she pauses only yince or twice yae down a dram or twa'.

3. Jeannie's no' a fashion chiel, dungarees are mair her style,
   She can hike a hunner' mile but can't see past her nose.
   Jogs tae work each mornin' in the city but on Saturdays
   She's out in tae the countryside tae bag a few Munros.

4. Campbell is the brother, he's a corrie haundit golfer,
   And he used tae play at fitba' tae his cartilage gave in.
   Turned oot for the Thistle, engineered his ain dismissal
   When he accidentally scored a hat-trick for the the other team.

A song about a ceilidh and its hosts. It could take place almost anywhere.

THE LASS O' GLENCOE

traditional arr. A. Reid
© Kinmor Music

1) As I was a-walkin' one evenin' in June all the birds in the bushes were singin' in tune, A lovely young lassie afore me appeared, the fairest of maidens that I've ever seen 2) Says I coe.

---

1. As I was a walkin' one evenin' in June
   All the birds in the bushes were singin' in tune.
   A lovely young lassie afore me appeared,
   The fairest of maidens that I've ever seen.

2. Says I "My young lassie you have a sweet smile
   And your braw, comely features my heart does beguile
   And if your affection on me you'll bestow
   I'll give thanks to the day that we met on Glencoe."

3. "Young man" she gave answer "Your suit I disdain
   For I once had a sweetheart, MacDonald's his name.
   And he went to the war about ten years ago
   And a maid I'll remain till he's back in Glencoe."

4. "Perhaps your MacDonald regards not your name
   But has placed his affections on some other one.
   He may not remember for all that you know
   The lovely young lass that he left on Glencoe."

5. "MacDonald will ne'er from his promise depart
   For love, truth and honour reside in his heart.
   And if I never see him it's single I will go
   But he promised one day he'd return to Glencoe"

6. So finding her constant I took out a glove
   Which at our last parting was a token of our love.
   She fell in my arms and she would not let go
   For she knew her MacDonald had returned to Glencoe.

7. Now he may be a hero or some nobleman
   Who has left his affections in some other land,
   The red storms of war in the distance may blow
   But we'll live here content in the pass o' Glencoe.

• Myself, John McCusker, Mike Katz and Davy Steele skulking in a back lane.
Would you buy a second hand car from any of these guys?

There are a few variations of this traditional song which has the oft found theme of long gone lover returning to find if his sweetheart is still hanging on for him.

On **'RAIN, HAIL OR SHINE'** - *See Discography*

THE WILTON STREET DAWDLE

Alan Reid
© *Kinmor Music*

For a time when I was a student in Glasgow I lived in Wilton Street in Maryhill. I wrote this tune then and called it 'Strolling Down Wilton Street'. But when I recorded it I slowed it down so the stroll became a dawdle.

On **'THE SUNLIT EYE'** - *See Discography*

SHE'S LATE BUT SHE'S TIMELY

Alan Reid
© *Kinmor Music*

An air written for the birth of our first daughter Morven. I arrived home from tour 12 days after she was due to be born. She very considerately, for me at any rate, delayed her arrival till after I got off the plane.

On **'ON THE RISE'** - *See Discography*

MARY CASSIDY

Alan Reid
© *Kinmor Music*

Written for my wife and partner of many years. Mary Cassidy is her maiden name

On 'HOME IS WHERE THE VAN IS' - *See Discography*

• Battlefield Band meet the steeplechaser named after them by leading trainer Peter Calver, of Ripon.

BRODICK CASTLE

Alan Reid
© *Kinmor Music*

Brodick Castle stands on the the island of Arran. It is more of a stately house than a fortification and has a beautiful walled garden. The tune is meant to convey a feeling of beauty and grandeur.

On **'MUSIC IN TRUST - VOL I'** - *See Discography*

A' CHLACH UAINE (THE GREEN STONE)

Alan Reid
© *Kinmor Music*

THE SLEEPING WARRIOR

Alan Reid
© *Kinmor Music*

The Sleeping Warrior
A tune I wrote for the Isle of Arran. When you view Arran, looking west from Ayrshire, the outline resembles a reclining figure with his hand across his midriff. The locals know this as 'The Sleeping Warrior', an image that has always caught my imagination.

On **'THE SUNLIT EYE'** *- See Discography*

A' Chlach Uaine (The Green Stone)
The island of Iona, where St. Columba established the first Christian church, is reputedly the burial place of around 40 Scottish and Norwegian kings. This wee tune is named for the green marble which is found on the island.

On **'MUSIC IN TRUST - VOL II'** *- See Discography*

CURSTAIDH'S FAREWELL

Alan Reid/John McCusker
© Kinmor Music

This is another tune I co-wrote with John McCusker, this time a slow air. It was named for my youngest daughter, who used to wave and say ta-ta in times of parting.

On **'QUIET DAYS'** - See Discography

CUMBERNAULD HOUSE

Alan Reid / John McCusker
© Kinmor Music

A fine slow air written by the the 18th century composer James Oswald

On 'THE SUNLIT EYE' - See Discography

GOAT FELL

Alan Reid
© Kinmor Music

A tune written for the T.V. series "Held In Trust" about the National Trust in Scotland. Goat Fell is the highest hill on the island of Arran and I wanted to make the tune sound the way I pictured the hill, spooky and grand at the same time.

On 'MUSIC IN TRUST - VOL II' - See Discography

FALKLAND PALACE

Alan Reid
© *Kinmor Music*

This is another tune composed for the T.V. series 'Held In Trust' where I wanted to convey an 18th century genteel classical feel. Because it's a keyboard piece and because it complements the right hand melody I have included the left hand in this transcript.

On **'MUSIC IN TRUST - VOL II'** - *See Discography*

SOMETHING FOR JAMIE

Alan Reid/John McCusker
© *Kinmor Music*

John McCusker and I dedicated this air to the birth of Jamie Steele, new born son to Davy and Patsy.

On **'LEAVING FRIDAY HARBOR'** - *See Discography*

• Me, perhaps looking fondly towards the beer tent on a hot day in Finland 1987.

THE CUMBERNAULD PERENNIALS

Alan Reid / John McCusker
© *Kinmor Music*

Written for a gardening club in Cumbernauld who invited myself and John McCusker to come and play for them.

On **'QUIET DAYS'** - *See Discography*

The Million Dollar Sweetie
There is a complicated tale behind this title, which involves a 'special' coloured sweet in packets of a major brand. If you found the sweet you won a big money prize. There is a possibility that our daughter Curstaidh found the 'sweet' but did what any seven year old would do, she ate it! But then she's one in a million.

On **'THE SUNLIT EYE'** - *See Discography*

Feiger's Warning
Written for my good friend Ron Feiger, now resident in Washington State. Ron at one time taught in Barrow, the northernmost town in Alaska, while attempting to run a laundromat business in Seattle, around 2000 miles to the south. In telling me about his grief with driers that kept breaking down and trying to get them repaired he urged me not to get involved in the laundromat business. I have followed his sage advice.

On **'THE SUNLIT EYE'** - *See Discography*

THE MILLION DOLLAR SWEETIE

Alan Reid
© *Kinmor Music*

FEIGER'S WARNING

Alan Reid
© *Kinmor Music*

ATLANTIC BRIDGE

Alan Reid
© *Kinmor Music*

I thought this tune must be in 3/4 time as I wrote it as a waltz. But written down it only works in 9/8 time, so there you go. I think it has an American feel to it, hence the title.

PINKY, PORKY AND JIM

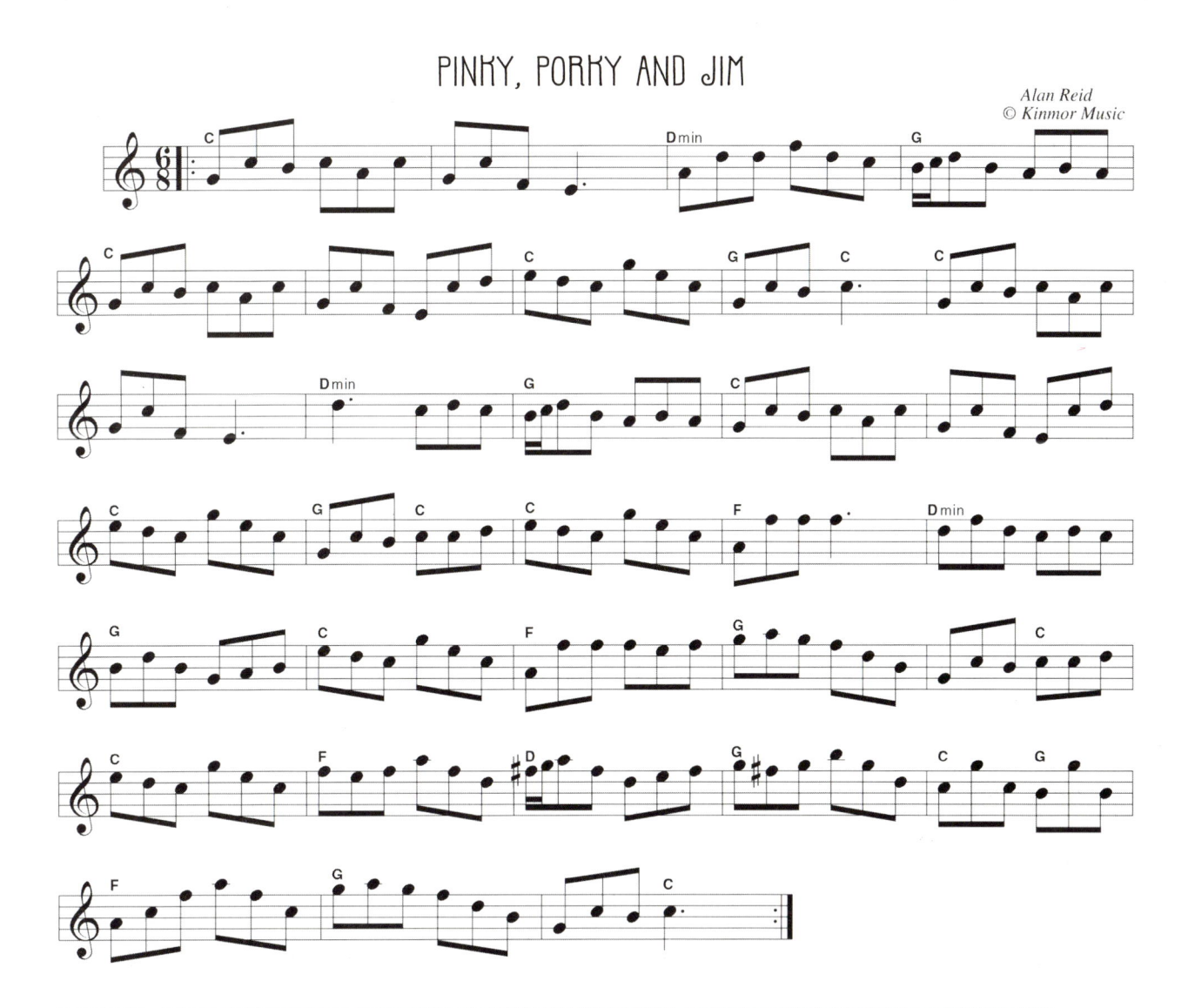

Alan Reid
© Kinmor Music

> I used to make up bed time stories to supposedly help the girls get to sleep. One of them was the *Three Little Pigs* and I started to add extra bits. Pretty soon the pigs and the stories took on a life of their own and became quite surreal and hardly sleep inducing. These are the names we gave them.

On **'THE SUNLIT EYE'** - *See Discography*

• Myself with Brian McNeill, Dougie Pincock and Alistair Russell in Kaustinen, on a tour of Finland in July 1987.

ANGST AGUS ANGUS

Alan Reid
© *Kinmor Music*

I have a weakness for bad puns and wordplay. I also have a friend called Angus who sometimes spends a lot of time debating with himself over very minor decisions.

On **'NEW SPRING'** - *See Discography*

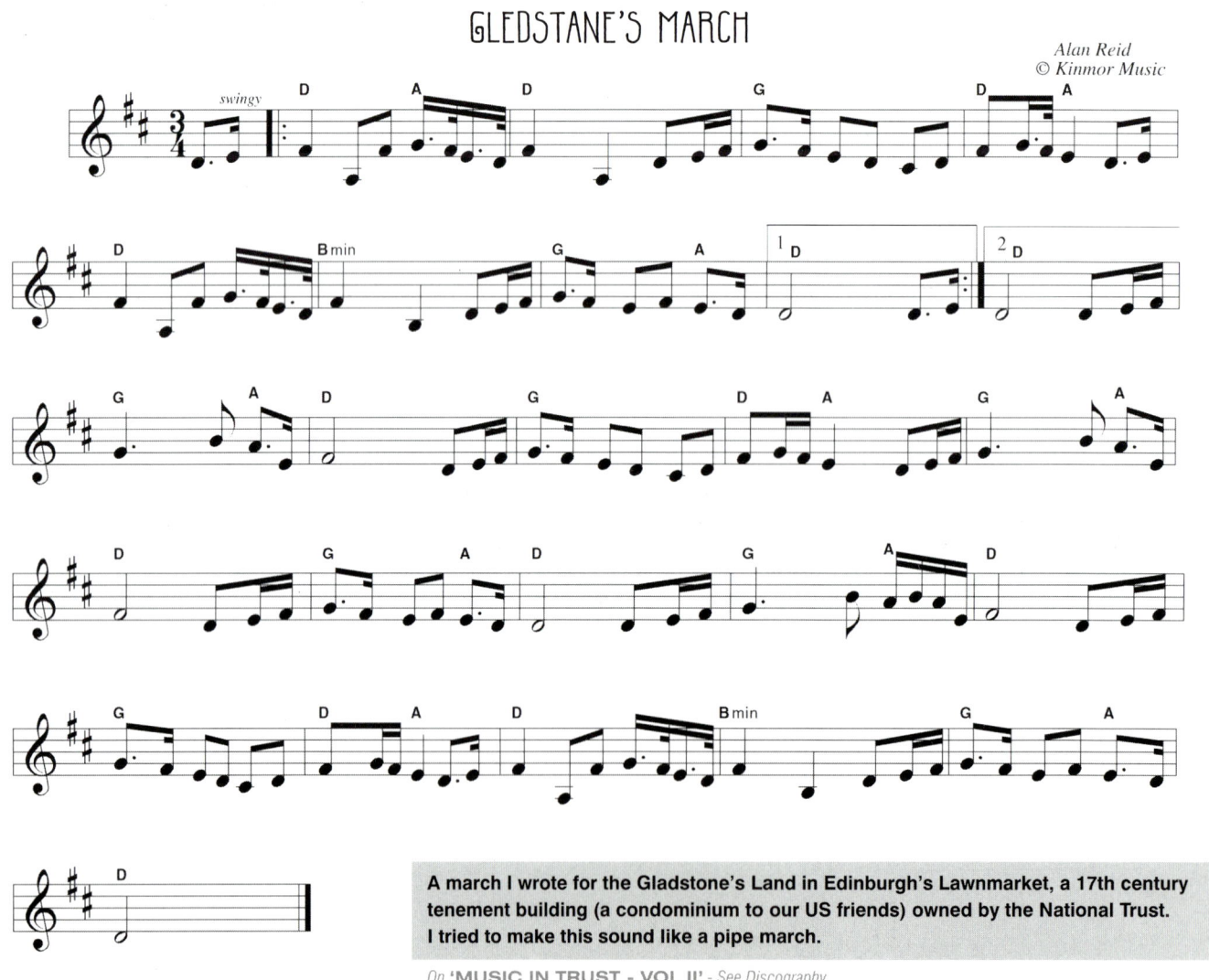

GLEDSTANE'S MARCH

Alan Reid
© *Kinmor Music*

A march I wrote for the Gladstone's Land in Edinburgh's Lawnmarket, a 17th century tenement building (a condominium to our US friends) owned by the National Trust. I tried to make this sound like a pipe march.

On **'MUSIC IN TRUST - VOL II'** - *See Discography*

RENALDO THE REBOUNDER

Alan Reid
© KinmorMusic

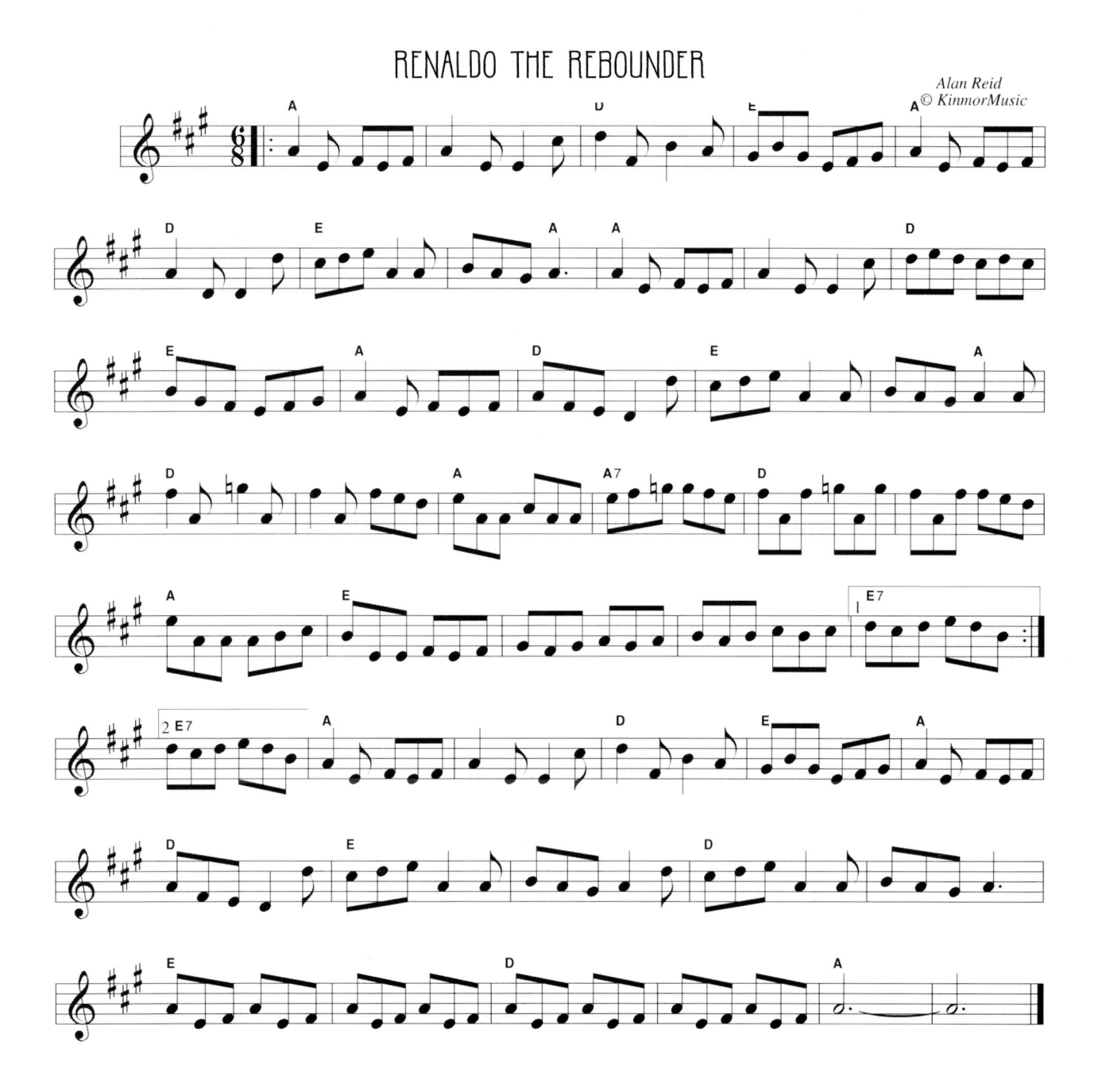

Many years ago I was hitch hiking around Europe and had reached Geneva. Walking in the summer evening I was surprised to hear the distant sound of the pipes. Following the sound I ended up by Lake Geneva, where a handful of people were watching a piper. He turned out to be from Gullane, near Edinburgh and was a trampoline artist in a local 'night club'. He planned to begin and finish his act by playing 'Scotland the Brave'. The club brochure had him pictured among a bevvy of exotic dancers with the legend 'Renaldo the Rebounder'. Renaldo, where are you now?

On **'THE SUNLIT EYE'** - *See Discography*

NORMAN MACASKILL OF LOCHINVER

Alan Reid
© *Kinmor Music*

• Relaxing in the Tass, an Edinburgh pub, during a rare break in recording the Happy Daze album, 2001.

A march written for a fine, hospitable gentleman and scholar, again with left hand included.

On **'THE SUNLIT EYE'** - *See Discography*

JAM TOMORROW

Alan Reid
© Kinmor Music

Have you ever noticed that we always seem to be promised jam tomorrow by the people who run the world. Nobody seems to get it today except for the privileged few. Or am I just being cynical?

LET THERE BE DRAMS

Alan Reid/John McCusker
© Kinmor Music

A reel I wrote with John McCusker and a sentiment that would be confirmed by quite a few folk that I know. Also a pun on a 60's instrumental hit.

On **'NEW SPRING'** - See Discography

DISCOGRAPHY

HOME IS WHERE THE VAN IS	1980	Battlefield Band	Temple COMD2006	
THERE'S A BUZZ	1982	Battlefield Band	Temple COMD2007	
ANTHEM FOR THE COMMON MAN	1984	Battlefield Band	Temple COMD2008	
ON THE RISE	1986	Battlefield Band	Temple COMD2009	
MUSIC IN TRUST - VOL. I	1986	Battlefield Band & Alison Kinnaird	Temple COMD2010	
CELTIC HOTEL	1987	Battlefield Band	Temple COMD2002	
AFTER HOURS (Compilation)	1987	Battlefield Band	Temple COMD2001	
MUSIC IN TRUST - VOL. II	1988	Battlefield Band & Alison Kinnaird	Temple COMD2004	
HOME GROUND	1989	Battlefield Band	Temple COMD2034	
NEW SPRING	1991	Battlefield Band	Temple COMD2045	
QUIET DAYS	1993	Battlefield Band	Temple COMD2050	
STAND EASY + PREVIEW (Re-release from 1979/1980)	1994	Battlefield Band	Temple COMD2052	
BATTLEFIELD BAND (Re-release from 1977)	1994	Battlefield Band	Temple COMD2055	
AT THE FRONT (Re-release from 1978)	1994	Battlefield Band	Temple COMD2056	
THREADS	1995	Battlefield Band	Temple COMD2061	
ACROSS THE BORDERS	1997	Battlefield Band	Temple COMD2065	
THE SUNLIT EYE	1997	Alan Reid	Temple COMD2072	
RAIN, HAIL OR SHINE	1998	Battlefield Band	Temple COMD2074	
LEAVING FRIDAY HARBOR	1999	Battlefield Band	Temple COMD2080	
HAPPY DAZE	2001	Battlefield Band	Temple COMD2085	

Other books published by
KINMOR MUSIC

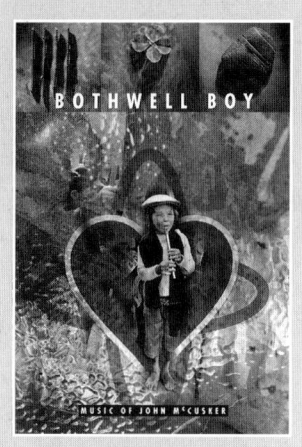

JOHN McCUSKER
Bothwell Boy
A collection of 56 tunes (some traditional) which have been composed by John McCusker.

BATTLEFIELD BAND
Forward With Scotland's Past
90 tunes & 44 songs (both traditional and original) from the repertoire of Scotland's top band.

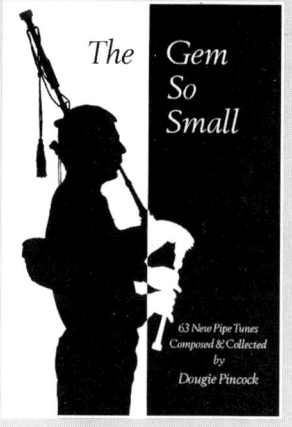

DOUGIE PINCOCK
The Gem So Small
63 new Pipe tunes composed and collected by Dougie Pincock. With accompanying cassette.

TEMPLE RECORDS
is our associated record label

Recent releases featuring Alan Reid's music and songs are:

HAPPY DAZE
Battlefield Band
COMD2085

THE SUNLIT EYE
Alan Reid
COMD2072

LEAVING FRIDAY HARBOR
Battlefield Band
COMD2080

These books and albums should be available through your local retailer.

Send for our full catalogue to:
Temple Records (Dept. AR), Shillinghill, Temple, Midlothian, Scotland EH23 4SH
Tel: 01875-830328 • Fax: 01875-830392 • Email: catalogue@templerecords.co.uk

All our books and albums are also available from the Secure On-Line Shopping Site at:
www.templerecords.co.uk

Check it out for special offers/new releases and up to date news of Temple/Kinmor artists.